Meet Me at the Happy Bar

a collection of poems by

Steve Langan

BlazeVOX [books]

Buffalo, New York

Meet Me at the Happy Bar by Steve Langan
Copyright © 2009

Published by BlazeVOX [books]

All rights reserved. No part of this book may be reproduced without
the publisher's written permission, except for brief quotations in reviews.

Printed in the United States of America

Book design by Geoffrey Gatza
Cover design by Janet Carkeek and David Helm

First Edition
ISBN: 9781935402534
Library of Congress Control Number 2009925632

BlazeVOX [books]
14 Tremaine Ave
Kenmore, NY 14217

Editor@blazevox.org

publisher of weird little books

BlazeVOX [books]

blazevox.org

2   4   6   8   0   9   7   5   3   1

B   X

ACKNOWLEDGMENTS

Thanks to the editors of the following journals, where some of these poems first appeared, sometimes in earlier versions:

Beloit Poetry Journal, Cimarron Review, Diagram, Drunken Boat, The Eleventh Muse, Fence, Hayden's Ferry Review, Hotel Amerika, The Iowa Review, Jacket, Meridian, Mot Juste, The Nebraska Review, Notre Dame Review, Octopus, Poetry Salzburg Review, Prairie Schooner, Slope, Sou'wester, Verse, Zoland Poetry

Several of these poems appeared in the chapbook *Notes on Exile & Other Poems* (The Backwaters Press).

Table of Contents

For Liz

Meet Me at the Happy Bar

Landscape with Pony

Landscape with pony.
Landscape with trumpet.
Landscape with underfed ponies and broken trumpets.

Landscape with promises.
Landscape with malcontents.
Landscape with syringes in a shoebox.

Landscape we've lived here so long clawing
after privilege you told me you would bring me
back to the sea before I die.

Seascape with promises.
Seascape with veterans.
Seascape with pink bikini and snowboots.

Variation on a theme by you,
variation on a theme by me,
and, in the evening, *Six Sonatas for solo violin.*

Self-portrait with potato farmers.
Self-portrait standing in front of the armory.
Self-portrait with the "old neighbors."

As brought to you by the Tube Socks Co.
Produced by Mr. Former Actuary Man,
directed by Mr. Stocking Cap all the time

and co-starring Sir Chemically Confused
with the one who usually plays the slut
and the Darling Child Growing Older

as the grave child with a tantalizing secret.

From the Earth

Give me just a minute to remember
the earth and what rose from the earth

beside you and me, to establish that in *dogged*
pursuit a passageway opened. Sacrilegious,

how the body currently responds...it *capers.*
But just after "congratulations" it swam away,

so tired of the pitchfork voice, obviously.
It was right there, the corpus, before it submerged.

A way of transgressing had been felt. A how-to
of not-feeling. Give me a second to remember

our beloved sun: in a box of chipped photos
we appear naked to the machines while rowing home.

Armamentarium

In the ghost-light especially children are drawn
to metal objects.

Some for sifting, some for conjoining or breaking in two.

At dawn nurses chat behind stained curtains.

When they discovered they had lost their fathers,
did they relax or did they press on more gallantly?

Was there a secret among rivals they were late to share in?

Did they sidle, conclude, long for, ache, protrude, mumble?

Were the boulevards from which they departed lined with
baskets of flowers, some hanging from railings?

Was indifference a flower plucked and worn in their hair?

Did magnitudes of thought (and erstwhile vocabularies)
venture into their *hearing*?

Did they recount the damned among them?

Was there some dulled semblance of an *anointing*?

Of a moment that refused to betray *permission*?

Studio A

How mere "pilfering" might play
under the klieg lights.

Petty theft.

An inch or two from the dire scene,
an inch or two in the other direction,
an inch or two off the top.

With words fit to place in your poem:
words, words, words, words.

Their edges are like silence,
can't you see?

Don't look at me like that,
stiletto of iron.

Same as the one you purchased
in Tijuana on Revolucion Blvd.

One goshdarn hot August afternoon.

—Suffer through this common form
of loveliness without a house
to call your own then you can come back
home by the fire and rest your crazy head.

A tortured reunion,
I'll put steaks on the grill.

Filet mignon,
and I'll invite the neighbors.

Look, redemption that fails.

Look, the failure of redemption.

Devastation at six o'clock
on the six o'clock news.

Study for an *Ars Poetica*

What am I listening for?

It's just like you to ask questions like that.

One word, one sigh too many, perhaps.

Disorientation spit out of the restless jawbones
of the owl.

The lyric of damages, with slivers of lightning.

Springtime, because we have survived our fits
and tergiversation again!

Our plenty—and *do laugh, my dear*, at how entwined
movement was with satisfaction.

Driving—or was it while walking from the motel
to the discount shop?—how I encountered a woman so similar

to one whom I had known previously, an uncanny presence.

—The sexual flowered. I took her in my arms
back by the radiator. It was that easy then?

The primacy of salvation…even for "people like us."

And I like how the rain comes sweeping over the heatstricken
bushes.

And the morning, how it enters and *dispels*.

Within the panic, a singing voice, rectifying space.

It comes forth, blends in, but is suspended.

"Go away sad song in love with the bones
around my heart"

as in a tunnel with neverending headlamps

working against the backdrop

each light singing *go away*.

Notes on Exile

They are wiping clean the fixtures with talcum.

Is it true what we say about the "healing virtues"?

You should not believe in all the properties of sunset.

This fine dance of opposites; a gossamer lunacy.

There's a hole in his heart about the size of her fear of death.

The fixed stare's upon us…can't you see it, arisen?

She is frightened she might enjoy the palliative.

"I don't mean to sound doomed and dreamy," he said,
"it's just the way the sun bends to her cotton nightdress."

What about the widow's unending declarations of innocence?

The mightiest fortress couldn't keep her home tonight.

There's a voodoo that registers in his mind I'll explain
next week at the annual function.

Recollections made whole, he stood still for plenitude.

This is my "art." These are my "patrons."

It makes perfect sense to him how the wind stole
the brush from beside the palette.

At a certain time in the morning day evening.

The clock sits atop the whistling prairie grass.

The time between now and harem.

Tinctures of dust, rusting ventriloquists.

Lateral desires, music straight from another galaxy near "heaven."

The worn and noxious husbands and soldiers.

Supremely moving disasters around the corner.

How could you blame him for trying to die?

What a shame, redress makes the future finally dry-eyed.

Don't you remember: he was the one *trekking*?

Or was it cobwebs or was it silver coils of hairlength?

You talk with people at parties. You know
what to say.

Rattle some pans to wake the status quo.

And while you're at it, knock loose some faith in the "Lord."

Wait, I didn't think we'd have to sing hymns all night.

Maybe we'll end up redeemers again after the blinds are drawn.

I don't know why we confuse kindness, oddness and science.

Do you have a plan, a tune, like iron and sunshine?

It is troubling to think of him lying in the basement.

It is frightening to think of him living underground.

Errant butterflies; winged tales of the sublime.

He keeps asking the matador to make sense of his cape.

All she ordered when I met her was the Denver Omelet.

The other overwrought survivors might "smile" occasionally.

Other than for his playing, Orpheus is known for suffering.

Wisdom: enchanter: tired of roadways, finally.

Then it was late morning, at the other edge of his cavern.

Succulence: unending: tired posters in a room that once held joy.

Pray for the relief from capitulation.

The beggars loved the misfits who loved
the ordinary patterns and the shadows.

"To borrow a line from a friend who fully understood
the teachings," the manual began.

I simply cannot commit to disaster and rooms full of treasure.

Filthy barricades, persuasive ranting.

If clarity were all they were after, why would they come
to this ivystreaked palace of light?

Another singer would be wailing by now.

"A veteran of song and screen."

Trysts of moonlight: failures of hearing: our excuses.

Love is finally an act of the mind, we learned,
in coercion with the timid hopes of the haunted.

I want to get my shoes back solid on the deck
then we can talk while we sail.

Cowls of sin, treaties of forgiveness.

The blankvoiced reasoner from the hemisphere of desire.

Furthermore.

Enlightened pilgrims at the shore made it simple: gifts.

Partly the rations, partly the filth, partly the lack of love.

Troubadours, bamboozlers, cowhands.

Troublemakers, vagabonds, the warped.

Incensed doubters in the corner booth.

Next to a pack of gesturers.

Order off the right side of the menu and you'll be safe.

Say once again "he is smiling" and I'll break this pan
over your melon.

On the beach, the same old promises,
lust and tomorrow, a baggie of barbiturates.

Empires of sound, the history of flight, roosting meadows.

A tricky symptom.

Like the "meaning" of the "broken glass."

In hallways, or into the fourth generation, or because of glee.

Suddenly, I had become a reshaper of stones
fabrics and whispers.

My art: decades of silence.

Over yonder.

Wait: the trays of salmon dips and springtime rolls
will make their way around the room shortly.

Generations of rust, declarations of fear.

She found an alter ego in the dust.

Squeezed and tugged till it was "love."

Siphon the gas so we have something to warm
our hands over in the morning.

Strip the flakes from the flagpole and repaint but first prime it.

Acolytes and disastrous rumormongers huddled
next to a painting of "August."

Hold on to some of those ideas, like the one about disaster,
reconciliation and promise.

Tatters, tidbits, trucks that haul the grand logs
of the Pacific Northwest.

Down the crooked wet highway.

We "made love" within the hollow trunk of the sequoia I remember.

At Redwood National Forest on the tour I remember.

A long way from home I remember.

Meet Me at the Happy Bar

In this corner, blood on a shawl,
and in that corner, representative man.

A bluebird dead on the hillside.
"*Bluebird*" or "blue bird"?

And how to describe its splayed plumage,
beak tipped in mud,
beneath the yellow-x'd oak?

Excess as a strategy against our dying?

After you finish your project,
will you meet me at the Happy Bar?

Moody interrogations or awestruck reminiscences?

"Somewhat closer to the heart of experience than usual,
but still not close enough"
is Paul Klee's epitaph.

Daylight's twittering details, as if from the broken jaw
of a parakeet.

(Nevertheless, one eventually tires
of the "talking component.")

(And seeing as you divulged it,
now your pet bird begs you by name for water.)

—A way to make the dust stop
in its descent under light, the mind
connecting some objects in the sitting room,
embracing some, rejecting others?…

Or a ritual involving talking into a megaphone
at the sunblazed boatyard
made exquisite, like a dollar postcard, by leaving?

Hijinks and Capers

That's a stupid thing to ask a broken man.
Stop thinking of clever things to ask me.
You bring your question in here
and make us look at it and roll it
between our fingers and place it on
the humming incubator's sterile slides.

How could such a structure *exist?*
Multiple structures twined with—
what is it?—elastic, confetti, birdsong,
blizzard? Would you trade even a moment
of bliss, or an afternoon of grandeur,
for these scuffed, worrisome garlands?

Ladies and gentlemen, attention must
be paid to the muse…like asking
vultures to the trees. Yeah, I'm talking
to you, slabs for eyes, casket for a brain.
Such an enviable set of disciplines:
so much science and precious little time.

But maybe there is time left to hum
in the celebratory manner. Is this one?
The answer is deer at the salt lick.
What I mean is rare coins and stamps.
I've heard rumor of a "dose of refinement,"
"pulses and animates," the "terrible whole"…

Hex

The wheel is angry and so is the blade.
Blue afternoon patiently umbers.
It is the word *contretemps* that hurts; the word
vicissitude. Beside me, the trained smile
even as she naps, webbed skin on her elbow,
the dilemma of a small, receding contusion.
I keep examining many of the passing items
but mostly myself in the beveled mirror—
when she is not looking—like a flashlight
trained deep into a well's awful opening,
an inch of sorrowful water, a piece of metal,
the whole summer's trapped thunder.

Buongiorno

It's my dirty little mind again.
Poverty, cunt, glimpses
sometimes of paradise.

Because around the farm
we're courteous and hardly
ever ashamed anymore.

Casual in interpretations,
painstaking in declamations,
steadfast.

At the check-point,
what were you asked?
About the road conditions?

What did you tell
the determined *carabinieri*?
About the mediocre pavement?

Let's get back to the subject.
Will you hold me a while?
Until morning.

And speak only in English,
please, in plain flat
stupid midwestern.

So I cannot forget you.

South Dakota

Is it always this quiet in Yankton, South Dakota?
The deer's head above the hearth—a *buck*.
Time is cadaverous.

With the key in the lock, just in case
she's returning.

And what belongings we brought with us in pouches
and bags, in a knapsack and arranged on the sink,
laundered on hangers and hung on hooks.

Promise you will not whistle along.
I have selected the *Piano Concerto No. 20 in D minor*.

It's a makeshift time capsule she holds between her knees.
Pearls, those kneecaps, in any weather.

This is a region that knows about suffering,
that's for sure. These good people
of South Dakota who have gone to all this trouble.

Let's pray they are safe and warm in their beds.
If I do fall to sleep and if I dream.

Meditation on the Cabin (and Beyond)

So what I haven't visited the ornate churches
or the picturesque lookouts to watch the sunset.

The horse is dead, the barn is shuttered.

Now who will tell us what we should read?

Said the doctor to his patient,
so much time and only one body.

You flash into my mind, dear one,
and are exalted then extinguished.

Safely tucked away, returned to exile.

All these forms of courage the mind enacts.

A wish followed by a denunciation.

Worlds apart, here's your world before,
here's your world after.

Ritual for three voices—
variations on desire, discontinuity, disgrace…

A song about ecstasy beginning *In the morning*.

With commentary on the stronger fixations, however.

In the book of seeing, it says release, it says *disengage*.

Lined up at the fence with light in their eyes,
look at em.

Psalm 22, *I am poured out like water,
and all my bones are out of joint.*

Maybe dilapidation serves as the model after all.

Meaning allowing the body its repetitive descents

and exhalations doubling and tripling downward
in three-quarter time.

Some guy re-sizing the world but giving in finally
to its recessed contours is a model.

She irons nude (and she doesn't want me to touch her?).

He seeks refuge in silence and artifice.

Sewing bits of wire over the holes in the window screens,

she keeps the mosquitoes out of the cabin,
that's her job.

He likes to wear his knife outside his clothing.

They have been seen in this jungle, through
this infrared scope.

Tending their property, and this is their property-line.

Lord and lady of the wilderness.

Uncanny, isn't it, the trees swaying to this music?

Said the priest to his penitent.

Said the vagabond to his bowl of soup.

Meditation on the Campsite and the Pier

These are some of the exotic lies we have told
to the shapes of the landscape.

Rocky formations surrounding handfuls of silt.

The campers looking crosseyed at the disassembled
rusty tent stakes.

I love you "everpresent" and focused on "learning
something new."

Doo-wop, the singer said as his sound-check,
and we were wakened from one pain to another.

Where we were once denied any form of sacrament,
here we lower our minds.

We lost everyone, each and every one of them.

They were on a path marked "Path."

What a sepulchral imagination you have…
we really must get together sometime…

The yellow flowers in the baby blue vase…
Forsythia.

These are my (wink) deranged friends.

If I promise they won't steal anything,
do you mind if they smoke in your house?

Now don't steal anything.

Imperfections, too, and boredom and fatigue
as part of the enterprise.

Not the wife's efficiency but the husband's gloom,
their hearts made of tin.

I'm new: why do I have to do everything around here?
Said the blue-eyed boy weeping for an aesthetic all his own.

A dense grief set in: the unflowering of the persistent
yet and *furthermore*.

Training the fishermen to be merciful to the boaters,
training the boaters to watch for their lines.

Try as they might, the cold seats at the harbor
are their home, fishing from the pier.

An ordinary person would be less impressed,
that's for sure.

A friendly clerk who told me to go one place not another.

Who elegantly steered me in the wrong direction.

Now look at the rods and reels and biblical imagery.

It's all biblical imagery.

Such as the objects, frail as they remain, of belonging.

—He admitted that while here he never belonged
to anyone or anything.

Admitted he was shoeless, that he had lost
his identification.

That he stared for hours at the waves and
cast at their sudden sharp tips until nightfall.

Vial

Vial broken inside the brain, *ahem*.
Slipshod, unrevealing powder.
Nevertheless, all my joints ache.
You don't need a license to *see*.

What kind of elegant branding?
Inefficient reckoning guides them.
All around us, the wires, flaming.
The windowsills, *amen*, are trained.

Tell me again about its plumage.
Remind me of the "satisfactory
reenlistment peekaboo game."
Via wilting lettuce leaves ascend.

Yellow-hued blunderers responded.
The voyage to the next station.
You cannot beat salvation.
No, you simply shouldn't miss it.

Stone (Where the Heart Is)

This city is perfect for us.
Every event is metamorphosis in reverse.
The buildings are glued to the earth,
the foreman whispers into his bullhorn.
I won't ask you to remember this place.
Who am I, anyway? Call me whatever you want.
And should the photos shock you, look away.
I lost one once.
She was sitting right in that chair
where you're sitting, Miss Jones.
Whoever said "Welcome" first was hailed "Master."
Whoever said, "There's no place like home"…
I simply cannot smile when I'm wearing the wrong clothes
so pardon my misery.
Any horse with Love in its name gets my money
across the board.
My little pot o' gold.
Next time you see me, I'll be behind the crosseyed
dice in the big silver car.
Stone where the heart is,
that kind of agreement seals a friendship.
Hurts, don't it? is a punching game.
At night he put away his two mad dogs,
our one-armed neighbor but he was fierce.
You just had to respect him.
Then an hour later the houselights went out.
That's when we knew we could relax,
drink some wine and watch TV.

Where Is the Cigar I Left Burning?

My glasses, wallet, keys?
The drink holder and the road
maps, cloves of garlic, Scotch
tape, the gas cans and my vitamins?
The jigger for your gin, my Lou
Reed CD, our last joint, my
letter sweater, the tickets
to the theatre, the journal
with the article I was reading
about the misconstruction
of deconstruction? The TP,
your famous IUD, the brochure
from the cemetery where we
can buy our plots now
so the kids won't fuss
or fight or worry?

Two-Parter

One
These frail barkers have sharpened windpipes.
The angry man is afraid of dogs.
So is the policeman. He cannot tell
his partner; she is enamored of him,
exiled, thoughtful, suicidal, coy.
Even the sexual lesson is hidden.
I've tried to be a good provider.
Long ago, I held her, my victim.
She looked so happy in cuffs I fastened
the leg irons; the antiquated need
for sympathy, then I brewed coffee—
it was late morning.

Two
All this is recurrring in the front
of the brain. *The Herald* is spread
on the floor. Sounds I heard,
stories, gestures, science, cosmologies…
I walk from bureau to bedside.
I'm going out for a walk. (Okay.)
Pick up some milk—skim. (I will.)
We whisper, we admire veterans,
recite halves of sonnets, try personae,
bake pork chops, yum yum, mushroom gravy.
Hold each other, rub shoulders, are victims,
bait, test atmospheres. All the while
the radio in the background, drum-beat
in the back-brain. All my life
the dial please to another station. (Driving
alone is better, for this reason and others.)
All this time the precise mood for the natural
humming to release—oh my God, I
said it, did they hear it, was it *true?*…

I hoped I could go on proving
this a fiction the teachers made us
start daydreaming at our desks,
in Mathematics, during Geometry,
drawing parallelograms
on light blue drafting paper.

Orpheus ("from a Certain Vantage")

But what will you do with your eyes, your damn eyes?
What to use the tongue for? the ear?
Tell us the sincere history of torture, heretofore unelucidated.

Do not turn around, young Orpheus, I'm begging you,
holding my breath, adjusting the lens, my back's to the light.
If I apologize for my part in the demise of love, will you?

Some viewers are singing, some fondly remember silence,
some are joking with the confused bagmen.
I need you to remember, Orpheus,

I need you to look into my awkward camera's throat
and say, "One cannot slave one's way into eternity, that's no joke."
She's wearing a red dress, her hair is filament and disaster,

she's cooing to the priests, the mothers, the strangers…
Do not turn around, weary Orpheus, do not sneeze,
signal, blush, do not leave a trail marked

with caskets of fear, rituals of pain, twilight cemeteries.

Eurydice ("from a Distance")

Speck on the other world, is your hood
pulled tight and tied? Blemish on this world,
wearing a raincoat walking in the rainstorm

is a good idea, say the wise. Mist is a baleful
procedure, how grass grows is a procedure,
both tree and squirrel follow procedures,

the lover disguises herself in procedure:
she raises the mainsail, she raises the jib.
Her soul is like that, a woman alone at sea.

Eurydice's in the distance, we cannot know
what she is thinking, she is following;
maybe she is humming then singing

against pain: thinking but declaring nothing
along the trail, whistling, remembering,
counting, then with sudden breath at his neck:

"Don't turn around, shroud of shrouds"…

Orpheus ("Perspective")

Just before or just after turning around?
Or in-between, one breath from the tape-breaking,
boy becomes man, finally, on the frontier, free gesture

sorrowful Orpheus can't take back because now she
is gone again, the beloved, it's been decided?
Maybe you wish to review the attending grieving,

as this may teach you better how to endure?
Or you prefer to watch the long hours of anxiety
filling his head before he yields to the inevitable gravity?

I can't deny your choice may lead you to greater
self-knowledge, etc. It could even make you stronger,
it could start to make you whole again,

studying the flickering restraint or self-torture.
But just so you don't forget, it wasn't his fault or hers,
yours or mine, we shouldn't blame God or nature.

The sun *was shining*. Beautiful Orpheus *turned*.

Reasons for Kindness

A kind of purity after all enters.
Stargazing (because we had been
shut-ins together). Accelerated
heart rate and breathing leading
to maladies if left untreated.

A store manager concerned
about employee retention, theft,
end caps. Eager beavers.
Society functions at which,
drunk on Chardonnay, you spoke
your mind. Reasons for kindness,
including but not limited to
beggars. Sheets hung to dry
on which there is also blood.

Are you able to condone sunrise?
Is kiwi the monumental fruit?
Trying to engage an old friend
is the reason he seduced his wife,
he said. Betrayal was the robe
her sadness finally made her wear—
apricot, gingham, in her quiet room.

One thing leads to another. I loved
them equally. We spent vacations
and holidays together. One morning
we all woke in each other's arms.

Good night peaceful little ones asleep.
Have mercy on our old neighborhood.
Behind the wheel of our shabby car
(on the way to the café then the arena).
Reasons for kindness, reasons for hope.

The Scarf

She made a scarf out of twigs and ash.

Obviously so much pain in the doubledecker morning.

Still, there was a risk factor, a series of
suggestions.

More remorse in the gray morning,
untitled gray lyricism.

Later, they stared grandly at one another
sloshing their soup spoons throughout.

Tell me again the story of the scarf.

It was made from iron and rusty crowbars.

From tongue and its fleeting monuments.

Because of the wanton spike wedged out of
the center of the failed topography.

Out of lip plus trance and its fallible *musica*.

She knit in the morning, in the evening.

Wedded to virtue, preternaturally
simple.

The scarf remained hung around the door handle
for everyone to see.

When you leave, even the deaf air screams.

Just once, but I swear I heard it screaming.

A Pact

Let's make a pact, a blood pact, that whenever
referencing the "old worlds" or the "new worlds"
we will designate them "the worlds" or "otherwise
known as the worlds" or "otherwise" or "O.W."

And while we're at it, with the sun at half-mast
and the moon and the gentle stars, when and if
they arrive, tipped so as we are dogs again
lapping what little light remains from bowls
lashed to the dirty earth, let's make a pact
in reference to "love" and one concerning
"time" and one more in honor of the soldiers
of the most recent war—in their brittle panic—
as if remembering facing down the enemy,
gaining a foothold, a flank and a front.

Let's make a wish, too, and let's not cry
at all, not one tear, even though the darkness
has arrived, you remember light, don't you,
and being moved to rapture by the singers,
their birdlike pronouncements in the final movement—

(shaking water from our hair beside the inlet)—
the glorious undisguised all at once *tweet.*

Elixir

Some fragrances lift both eyelids
to the windless sunlight in the morning
same as any enraptured or wounded
human awakes. And though it's the answer
to a child's urgent query, today
I must have been placed here to tell you
there's a hill in Port Angeles, Washington,
as cohesive in its untrammeled colorations
as *the surf must have felt against the raft*
lifting the three survivors to shore…

I've rarely been stranded, never starved,
just quiet, *hushed*, privileged, with a few
hallucinations, and cantankerous sometimes;
now, so you might hear from the other room
as I pull the stained, scratchy afghan over
my deep faith in discipline and silence,
I hope to tell you again, regardless,
a rambling narration of the illogical grasses
on the hillside you did not see, dear one—

and beg you to forestall our honed martyrdom.

I Was Young Then

I had no idea your heart was sick
or that you were reputed to be
a number of sinister things,
a reptile soaking in privilege
and spitting out desire, for instance.
I was building a platform from which
I could speak of the holy phantoms.
The orchestral background frightened
and soothed. Sorry for being touchy:
the slightest movement could have
thrown off the entire system.

One morning a bird carrying
instructions rolled into its talons
landed on the bank of the river
I could see from the window by
which I sat to drink my coffee.
Beneath me my faithful dog rose,
howled, and scratched at the door.
I let him outside and—his trainer
and master—motioned to the trees
and the water and demanded *Kill—
or don't you come back here again*!
The air went with him, and the night,
and the night after that and the moon.

There is part of me that is molten lava about this.
And there is the lava bubbling to cool part.
Call me "Landscape with Animal in the Foreground,"
a deer or coyote whistling static, inhale and exhale,
alert but daydreaming freeways of pastureland.

Part of me is lava baked into a cake, candles a-blaze.
Use your finger, like this, to smooth down the frosting.
Elsewhere, deer graze,
birds are returning, shoots sprout beside the trailhead—
sounds of green, smell of shine, a boot-print in the mud…

—Early afternoon, mid-October, political signs shrug and cower
in the breeze. The counter-top is lava, the clock-radio is lava,
nostalgia is lava with our initials gouged out.
Call me "Landscape with Roosting Birds,"
call me "Landscape with Whispers."

Movies

I am not so eager to die again today
but I often enjoy watching the current movies

such as the movie I watched last night
starring your favorite actor and my favorite actress

whose lines dusted the shelves of longing,
emptied bric-a-brac onto the mantle,

then chased away invaders with a flare
and a broomstick all in a day's work.

When the movie ended, I was thinking
of death, and though I swore

I would stop thinking so much about death
and the undergrowth of mania, the meaning

of stars and the ambiguity of forgiveness,
I lay in the starlight of the TV for a while—

in the melody of the rolling credits—
considering death and madness and love—

soon under the spell of the arbiters of panic
who know better than to rename need.

Notes on Silence

These *gusts*. Irreversible motives. Encroaching
eagerness.

Though not as eager to confirm reportage
of previous symptoms.

Here's something you wouldn't want to find
wrapped under the tree (*heard upon approach*).

Some memories were indeed explored.

The sideways items must wait for another blue day.

Such as sermons from hilltops with exaggerated claims
and shoulder-length hairdos.

Remarks, quips, innuendos; treaties drawn up
on napkins.

This is one of the kinder ways we encountered the *silence*.

Friend, it's been so long since we talked this way.

Bonhomie, transcendence, patiently; plain,
level and true.

At the five corners the aquifer regenerates.

Which serves as proof of not just one but both fists
pounding on the dashboard of the Fiat.

When I cross the river (the river *yawns*) it's thirty years ago.

Notice how the enchanted heron rises and she just
nodded at us.

The gasoline truck fills the afternoon with its logo.

You really need to "get out of here." You need to
"expand your horizons."

At dusk in, say, Lithuania, the water towers
developed by Stalin for his modernist hovels.

The alleyway smokers relish quietude, too.

Haven't you heard her sing, that little mouse of a girl?

Tell me what's the best revenge, again?

I wasn't thinking of you at all. Well, maybe a little.

7:21 on the digital clock-radio.

The slats and shades measuring the variables of silence.

Thieves and hoodlums disrupted our fun party.

They placed a *hex* (see previous display) upon us.

Time sewn into our lapels;
time sewn into our entire wardrobes.

Now by other rules they are trying to own your mind.

Now in another way they have sewn shut your eyes.

Don't mind them.

It wasn't that they *couldn't have stopped* or that they
have been forgotten or that it *lessens much.*

It's because fancy directives lie unburdened
in their repertoires.

—They had a conference before they came in to disarm us.

In one way, they were dehumanizing the inevitable;
in another, something precious was held up to ruin.

Among the muddle and the balm and the muddling
songs of the birds at the trough.

I cannot—I really should not—suggest a sojourn
then orientation toward detail.

Regardless, don't you want to hear the sad lipstick songs?

The chanteuse who in her ear magnified desire?

Among the runaways and the men living in boxcars?

The chanteuse singing and the rail cars breathing?

—And what are you made of, really?

Into that microphone right there, tell me. Say it.

Can you see that now is your big chance?

Would you want to wait your entire life?

Itchy Poem

to itch; not to scratch

the wrong modifier; wrong tense

part of the fuselage; the o-ring

two deer; two deer mating

here; and why I love living here

twilight; an old woman wails

the train passes; waving from the caboose

an unintended look; a smirk

you don't come to see me; I'm lonely

my house: some boards, some sticks

to love; meaning absolutely

here in paradise; here in this fortune

a bird lands: stupid bird

a bird lands: lovely bird

plumage; my weak, tired body

alone again; it's midnight

a dog barks; a gate, latched

a car alarm; some footsteps, now fast

wet; slapping

On Your Eyes

Beautiful.
Different than on TV.
(To have her love you
repeat after me.)
1. Sociopathic eyes
2. Depakote eyes
3. Fill in the blank eyes.
Or friendly, inviting.
Thoughtful (meaning autistic?).
Thoughtful (*depressed?*).
Mercurial, symptomatic,
hiding something,
contrary, "on fire,"
under pressure.

___________, who never looked me
in the eye. Who stole from us.
Overwhelmed.
Like the eyes of a bully.
Barely a thought in his head.
And that's how meaning works:
you forget stuff.
Touched with greatness,
held up as an example,
cerulean.

Remember, the one
            who forgot
to write and send
the thank you note?
He winked at the interviewer, too.
The *gall.*
A rare spirit
            (he told us
            he fell asleep
            afterward
            in the parking lot)
whose eyes were either
hazel or noncommittal.

Epidemic

Not from your country,
I'm a survivor
of the war in your
countryside. Now I
stand and ask "Do you
want your eggs scrambled?"
when I should be asking
"If we think long and
hard enough about
all the lost blood and
skeletons and talk of
reincarnation,
how can we kneel
on this hard floor, on
our tender kneecaps, to
forgive, among
others, ourselves?"
Is this a poem for
young men who die from
love and the body's
reconciliations?
Or is there a deaf
beast behind this thin field
of sighs who fears us
as much as we ignore him?

So what should we do about father?

Because it's midnight,
tell us the story of the wanderer.

If he ever mentioned the air raids,
that was friendship.

And if you place all the pills
one on top of the other

and turn on the lamps,
you can see to Plattsburgh.

Mother laid on the sex appeal
sometimes.

Also, there's a spring that needs
to be wound; I read that

in the manual.
Father worked at the airfield.

It's time to go (in secret)
to the after hours club.

There's a novel you should read
by the Spaniard X.

It helps with perturbations
such as these:

slow perusal followed by
full-fledged meditation.

On our coat of arms
is a woman in a lawn chair.

I drew it while I
was at my second job.

Let's allow father to take
his place in heaven.

If he doesn't remember,
so much the better.

Then allow
his cap into heaven

and these utensils,
his unintelligible ledger

and his fine teeth while grinning.

To My Friends

I have wanted for us to catch up.
From here, a heavenly monotony.
What was feared, as it arrived,
what the ancients proscribed,
after reading the haters and hooligans,
in communion with star *and* wave.
I'm just a little boat tied up beside
a cliff—a *dinghy*. I'm sure you remember.
The last twenty years or so?
House, house, house, cars, many dented.
Dinner with the in-laws. I'm *married?*
And all our children crying at once
and hungry *shut them up and feed me.*
If there was beauty it was not caring
about clearing the counter tops ticking
beneath the clocks, alert on the shelves.
On to us. One day I sat up straight.
Metaphor, from the Greek: *to transfer.*
There is even some mystery here
in Nebraska. It's Friday morning.
The neighbors are speaking to me again
(*Hullo!…Have a good one!*) and so are
the robins. I sat still one day. I had been
so silent. I remembered you all, slouching.
In the rear view mirror, your faces, aching.
I realized you would one day be dying.
I walked to the window (at which I have
been reminded *you are not an old man
who is dying!*). At the spigot, I checked
the attachments. I searched for progress
throughout the materials. I shook hands
with the governor, I called on the warden.
A priest smiled "not *at you*," Liz said,
"but in our *general direction.*"
I hung my wardrobe (by color and weight).
I nodded at my brown shoes and black shoes.
I looked out the window again. I searched
through the grass for the necklaces I knew
I would not find and did not find them
then it rained. For seven days ten years ago

I never told you I believed I was the savior.
For many moments in thrall or wailing.
For three days I planned to murder her.
Had I been trained too well *to believe*?
—*A plane overhead.* I'm in my backyard.
No…a helicopter. Allow me to reconsider.
Let's meet at the bandstand in September.
I always love September. Bring at least
seventy sunsets, twenty pipe wrenches,
forty broken windows. You will remember.
I was drowned and scarred and scorched.
Will you call me? You can count on me.
I will not omit triumph or disaster.

Enough reminiscing—our ears are melting.
I hope they cut the cake so we can go home.
A quiet pose, intermediate but graceful.
I'm a dusty coffin since I met you.
Thank you, moon, for staying the same
as the night we met; thank you, stars,
for christening then allowing the gala.

There are quieter theories, a worn repose.
A soft and especially wet kiss on the mouth,
his hand on your back guiding you in the door.

Pay him no attention. He was the neighborhood
bully. Undocumented, suffering lapses,
certainly he's come a long way,
but he's still dangerous. A catch in the throat,
a flaring of nerves, fatigue, exhaustion.

Nevertheless, at the carnival he smiled
at a baby. But when the mother handed
her baby to him, neither was sure of the hour.

The Photograph of Edna's Choir

Edna feels okay, she walks with a cane,
she's built a quaint chapel in her throat
where the filtered strains of unrequited
glances and payoffs glimmer.
It's her light source, her ritual dream,
the chalice held on high, spartan altar,
eyes closed. It's built on her tongue—
brick, metal—on her gold molars,
in the tiny mirror: wipe the mist
to the uncracked light,
open for spray, lean and spit, rinse…

Edna's long-defunct choir in its drenched
robes is jubilant, steady gazing,
within this panoramic view: individual ovals
circle like errant notes to be added
later to the score, with no names anywhere.
Their indistinguishable smiles make me
dizzy; they know all the words by heart—
and what did the photographer finally say
to make the choir look at him like this,
so proud, with imperceptible regret?

If we were to leave this Hall of Mirrors
with two mirrors in it and nails and shards—
our misshapen halos melting down our shoulders—
and go out driving into the yellow traffic,
would there be silence or tears enough
to let us find our way out or *home?*

—In the morning, a thousand balloons rising
from a field are another anointing. A young man,
a worker, and an older man, his partner…
the difference between a laugh and a belly laugh.
Will lucky azaleas in the Garden District bloom
for the lovely women of Dixie waking to their homes?

—Last night, John had a dream you married a Muslim
and moved to Beirut (consult dream books).
John, the wise one, and *you*, though struggling
to release from the overburdened self
the ceremonies it carries, are *in pain*. It's not even
past, the past. *Welcome*, your dog barks, *home*—

what can I do for you but sleep and dream
in your holy lap, this unbelievably warm throne!

Good Fortune

Again, she mentions our good fortune.
This is the life, isn't it?
Some foliage we walk through gives off gas
or is it heat? Some rocks are jagged,
some are centuries smooth for skipping.

*

I come here often, this path to this beach.
I like to pick up the thin almost-translucent rocks
and place them on my sifting plate
and later into the Mason jars I seal
to set atop all the windowsills.

*

Back at the cottage, I hold her a while,
then move way too fast
forward all the while thinking thoughts
and not even taking time to put on
some music. "Our song"?

You had to ask.
Give me one more second.
I'll remember.
                    Help me.
Hum.

Fifths

Maybe after all these years
you would like to be broken
into fifths?
Your features multiplying,
five pairs of glasses
atop five broken noses,
and your mouth—
slightly downturned since
the separation—times five.

After all the worrying
over the rent and the time
you backed over Billy's bike
(I just know I screwed up
Billy), maybe you're finally
ready to be broken into
five sections then
reassembled with looping
stitches that entered
like a sound you forgot
to keep listening for.

Or maybe you'd prefer
to be transformed into
a confection, a tasty treat
on a platter full of crumbs
and thumb prints presented
to you and your sad little
date on a Wednesday evening
in Grand Island, Nebraska,
with theatrical precision.

In Maine

Pain is a crude emotion; for instance,
the pianist who cut off his own finger
like a frayed length of line…
which is how I was reminded:
motoring to the Island
down an alleyway of moonlight,
thinking I admire his nearly superb
playing still, his resoluteness
concerning disaster and rejuvenation…

But what good are heroes anyway?
every stern lobsterman and lobsterson
and daughter seems to want to say…
and what if the lobster family
has it right: as you hurtle forward
bearing your undeniable gift,
your mediocre, praised playing,
into the cautious motif of your elders,
their stark wallpaper, fearfulness?...

Would you forget your lessons, your Every
Good Boy Does Fine? Would it be about
enough to make you forget the invention
of jazz—it's a sound and style
that represents a nation—your toes
tapping inside your better shoes?

Lighthouse Poem

Someone said "I've been cut" but where's the blood?

Each branch—I mean each leaf—on my neighbor's sycamore.

Not forgiveness (in the garden, in the stadium).

Not the stain-on-her-dress or litanies
or ransom notes.

"Muse, guard at my family door, under the flaky moon,"
the letter began.

There's a thumbprint in the middle of her photo
but so be it.

Later, in the anteroom, the veterans will counsel
you on disaster and recompense.

A befitting memory
(like "the crack of the bat").

Of course this is a neverending puzzle,
just like time.

The Deer Crossing sign; the Boulders Falling sign.

He blessed himself with black ash
(rainwater mixed with leaves from the gutters).

He was reverend for a day.

Could we remember to finally be *elegant?*

These lights
and the shapes of the other possible lights

and the lightning in the voice of a girl
you could've loved—had you spoken—*said some words.*

This poem ends "at a lighthouse"
(or with a memory thereof).

Skyward, onward, holding open their mouths
to catch the raindrops, bless them all.

1959, the family came down from the lighthouse,
technology begins.

Quietly, charged with life, consider
the shape of the sky in the other city.

You've just got to give me the number of your designer.

The man in the spoked suit; the one in the spoked tie.

In vain the buzzard houses herself with the sky.
                    (Walt Whitman)

Cicadas have no life outside of their desire.

—Lucky gems, vastness presses, superimposes.

And the cicadas appear to be staring down at us.
                    (Socrates)

Blessed cicadas, I thought the universe was *free*.

Self-portrait (yesterday, at rest).

In here,
some books and magazines, a picture of a train,

and her eyes: two question marks aspiring
to be commands.

There, separating the bay, that's Halfway Rock
(this is a *real place*, listen).

Self-portrait ("insomniac with the four-second delay
of light"),

and this is a real place, noisy one, so *listen*.

Halfway Rock *it is on the chart*
(give them latitude and longitude).

Not far from Ragged Island, Maine, where Edna
St. Vincent Millay wrote and drank.

Drank and wrote.

Who appears in *The Book of Lists*
as one of the "top twenty famous drunken writers"…

And was said to have stirred the imaginations
of men.

Her poem about the candle,
her great poem about *mercy*.

The Book Finally with All the Misery in It

The book finally with all the misery in it.
The epigraph's crossed out, so is the appendix;

so is the sentence with the chorus
from the song we played thirty times a day

in 1989. I'm already tired of this century.
Mothers, children, their forgetful children.

I can't keep them all straight. We walk
into the arboretum for solace and inspiration

but that's not it—that's doesn't do it at all—
and the racetrack doesn't need me anymore.

The tavern where we pronounced ourselves
man and wife doesn't need us;

the corner where the jukebox sat,
with my hand up her blouse, is a bare table.

The book with all the words I've
neglected to say to the mothers and children,

including misery and finally. Or the book
with the mother and her child and they're happy

or at least smiling in the photo on the back
cover of the book finally of misery

I've been telling you to read and, when you
won't read this book, I read to you from it.

The book of the dainty and the dead.
First chapter, dainty. Final chapter, dead.

And in between, irascible thieves broke
into our apartment, which gave us a story

to tell to our group of friends,
all of whom then shared their stories

of misery finally at the going away party.

Great Joy

And even, at times, great joy,
repeats the trained parakeet.
Somebody please behead the little monster.

—Have you ever met one of those
everchanging persons, a brand new persona
for each half decade or so, with a reined in

crazy streak, but still so beautiful, so stunning,
you want your friends—your new friends
and your old friends and people whom you haven't

befriended yet—to meet and know and love her
as you do, fitfully but with no violence?…
"What I hear is the therapy's working,"

said Ivan, and I don't want him carted off
to the gulag for thinking then saying it,
the smiling wincer, the wincing smiler

from the Monday evening *group*,
because maybe I have settled into the dull logic
of peace and love, finally, just maybe.

—So how do you explain the rage toward
your friend's pet bird as you twirl
his delicious pasta to the profound jazz—

his scraggletopped pupil and mate,
the one he calls forth to be audible,
unforgettable and even tame

for you and only you to applaud then vanish from.

Apricots

In your note you asked for apricots
in the silver dish. I brought you apricots,
crushed, pureed, in the gold decanter.
You wrote they are delicious,

the chilled apricots, jellied, *untamed*
I wrote back it is marvelous that you enjoy
and do not fear the full glass
set before you on the bare counter

and that you mention it now
in a fine cursive lacking its usual panic.

Talisman

Family pet with her bum hind leg,

I've grasped colorful tatters before
wound into elaborate neckerchiefs,
and we went walking through the park
holding hands whistling a song from before
despite our awkwardness at aging.
Recriminations finally weren't enough.
For a while I carried an ice pick
in my jacket pocket for protection.
Every straggler's a potential foe.
Sometimes for no good reason
I've been kind though. I wanted to,
but I didn't slice a one of them.
Everyone finally knew I'd been away.
How far? The frontier of the skyline,
the top row of the stadium, underground.

I continued looking for satisfaction and,
exhausted by repetitive chance encounters
with my betters, became withdrawn.
Only Marguerite Fernandez, who served us
the best huevos rancheros here in Boise,
seemed to understand me. My appetite
remained steady, I was losing my hair,
I did the crossword in the corner booth.

Transparent, left on filthy stoops,
we come into the world as burden
and remain pitiful sacraments on the altar.
Our chores make us eager vagrants:
taking the trash can down to the tree belt,
clearing grandma's boxes from the attic.
Guarantee me, feeling feeble this afternoon
and maybe you've felt feeble today, too,
that being remembered for dutiful sacrifice
is the sorriest memorial of them all…

and that, while attending the service, I was not
the one who revealed his glorious caprice.

History of a Town

Was there a proper way to recline
on the empty bandstand?
I sometimes miss solitary menace.
It went on like this: soundings,
wannabes circling the square,
cruising the strip, buzzing the gut.
Everyone west of 99th Street
wants to eschew the historical.

You don't have to believe in their demise;
you've just got to believe they're still out there.
There was a surplus of majesty once.
The exceptional pert little tattletale
in her father's Buick Riviera, for instance.

I drove us by them. Gas was cheap.
As a toddler the psychopath
will not *point* (at cars, at balloons).
I've had significant secrets and those
less apt to restore me (after all
the self condemnation and peeling
the layers of shame and guilt).
I was always known as an observer.

At the gas pump the attendant
wearing boots and beads is not afraid
of us nor are we afraid of him.
Alone at the counter waiting for
a BLT there is time to remember
the alien promises—rescue, renewal.

Avoiding hysterical responses we continue
into the quotidian, stopping by the park.
We watched the crew film some
propaganda on Spring Street. It was fun.
Nightfall meant something at last.

It takes nerve, gumption and moxie
to remember all we've been through
and document it for the next generation.

If you don't believe me, ask your neighbor.
Unspeakable situations are abundant.

They ripen on the vine but sickly,
one could say, but I wouldn't believe
such a transparent approach to nature.

I suggest you ask several of your neighbors
and combine their responses to formulate
an hypothesis or a comment on our culture.
Ask your neighbor with the leaf blower
or the one walking her Jack Russell Terrier.

I don't really know just how the questions
should be presented, but I have little doubt
about the responses, says the salesman in me.
You just have to believe in the suffering
of others; it's really the only way
some of us can go out into the new day.

Notes on Landscape

The landscape—this new landscape—resolving itself.

No more than four of you on that side of the picnic table
or it'll topple over.

He's a little guy, just a speck of grease and noise.

Born to stroll in quiet weather, just looking around.

In his old loafers with crust on his lips.

Swirling trajectories, remembered sciences, ultimatums.

This day's composite: nipple, bowl, spoon…

Some boys have gathered in the storefront light.

With a mind of winter, one is looking at a looking-glass.

One is smoking, one is pacing,
and the synchronized breathing of the others.

Adequate strut, mean visage, distribution of fierceness.

It's the barometric pressure;
it's an affliction of the inner ear.

I handed you a packet of rice to throw at the moon.

After you tied iron and silver to the daring bride's car.

Along the way, singing and telling many lies.

Hurling our pain from the sidewalk into windows left open.

Every action in its rhythm, hallelujah, set us free!

Each excruciating blade of grass in its rhythm.

And the wind, too, regardless of what you have heard.

There goes a rat, past a fresh puddle of drool.

Salvation is a mouth with fine hair on its gums.

There is no other way but the sky. Focus.

There is no other way but the ridge. Listen.

The sun is pounding its fists at the low-flying birds.

Who are unbecoming to the rain-devouring roses.

With fish of all kinds curling up to die at the tide-line.

Ninety degrees today, could be a hundred tomorrow!

Pictures of miscarriages float past, a highlight reel
of devastations.

I swear I'll be home as soon as I wipe down the bar.

Only answer to our "secret-knock-with-the-doorknocker."

A horse slowly comes out of the trees,
a patch of mud under its left eye.

I have warned you about walking by yourself
out there.

I know it's a *drawing* of a horse but its mane looks
so real.

I must have told you a thousand times not alone.

Ceremony

Look at the names on the psychic blackboard
(it hangs on the wall, it holds all the names).
The excruciating (because of the wisdom)
villanelles with dates and leaves
stretching backward, ivy for the mind,
vines for the body, a jar on the hillside.
Not fatigue exactly and absent of anguish,
a lavender silence during which one is unaware
has brought you and some others to the ceremony.
From the tub she says, "Jiggle the handle
so the toilet stops running," the cruel pipes,
running her hand over the polished panels
while waves settle memories of torture.
And other imprints: time and space, for instance?
scenes to be averted? bouquets by the van-load?
imprimaturs in the dust and rust?…the ceremony
as it calls forth the next participant and the next,
as it "plugs along," ceremony of the wise earth
skipping past some items, emphasizing others,
and like Keats who wrote, "I am a coward…
I cannot endure the pain of being happy,"
in the pews of bent posture mild children cough.
They rattle in the windless orchard. They blush
and whiten and look like themselves. Detention
with staring guards, ceremony of the shine
off their barrels, the excruciating (because of
the wisdom) plea of the choir's progression,
the momentary unresurrecting surfacing
of small faces sharply and finally glancing.

Coda

Punched me hard, tried to push me down the stairs,
sang at funerals in a brilliant whine that made us
weep, clutch, lash out…genuflected round the fire,
blocked out mystery most times it entered,

was fearful of odd things like processions
and garlands, promised to begin to live better,
chuckled fondly at remarks made by confidantes,
and once said, "What bright idea do you have tonight,

Mr. I Don't Listen to the Blues Much Anymore,
Mr. Trumpet Blown Deep into the Crosswind?"

Made in the USA
Monee, IL
08 July 2026